WINE
JOURNAL
TASTING
AF225171
THIS BOOK BELONGS TO:
CONTACT INFORMATION:
NAME:
ADRESS:
PHONE:

Place Label Here.

WINE

Name

Vineyard

Country • Region

Grapes

Type

Alcohol %

Price

Serving Temperature

Purchase Location

PEOPLE

Location

Occassion

Names

APPEARANCE *(Circle One)*

RED	Purple	Ruby	Garnet	Tawny	Brick
WHITE	Amber	Pink	Gold	Brown	Yellow
ROSE	Red	Pink	Salmon	Copper	Orange

AROMA *(Describe smell such as fruits, herbs, and spices)*

TASTE *(Describe the sweetness, acidity, tannins, and body)*

NOTES

Place Label Here.

WINE

Name

Vineyard

Country • Region

Grapes

Type	Alcohol %
Price	Serving Temperature

Purchase Location

PEOPLE

Location

Occasion

Names

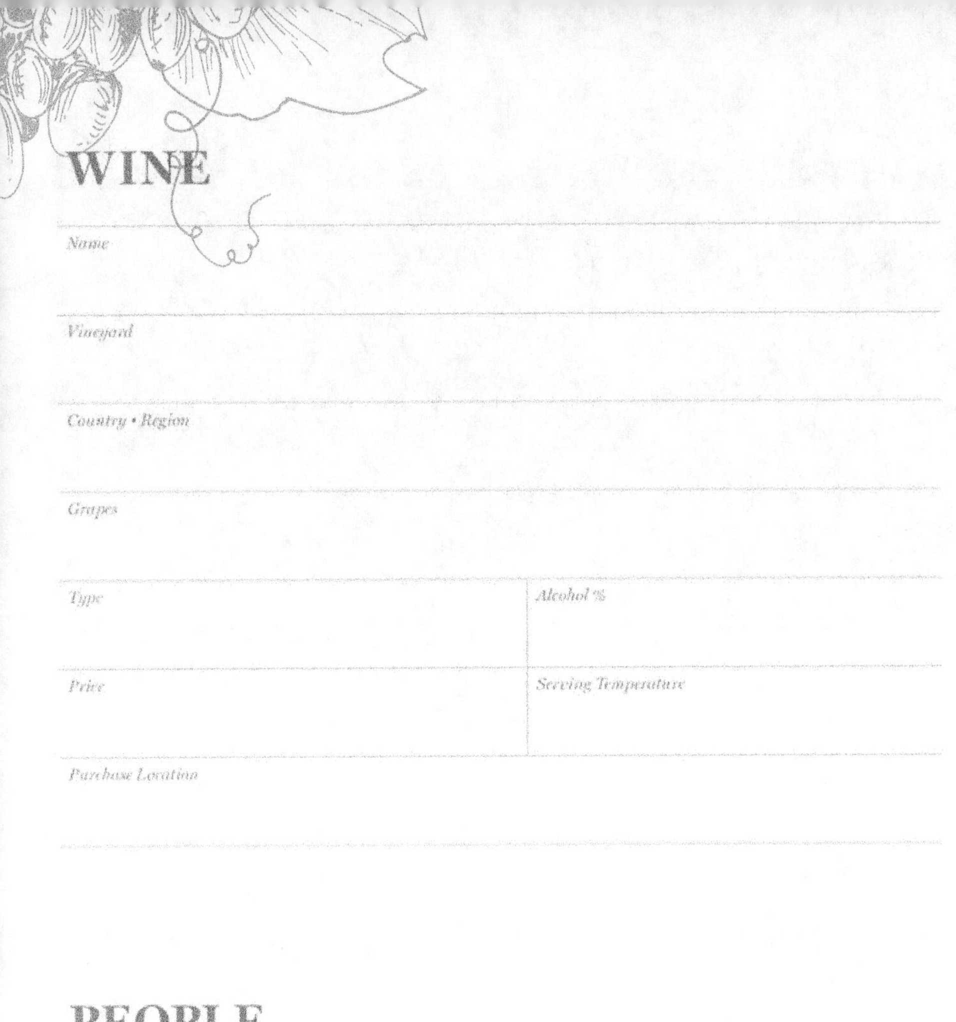

APPEARANCE *(Circle One)*

RED	Purple	Ruby	Garnet	Tawny	Brick
WHITE	Amber	Pink	Gold	Brown	Yellow
ROSE	Red	Pink	Salmon	Copper	Orange

AROMA *(Describe smell such as fruits, herbs, and spices)*

TASTE *(Describe the sweetness, acidity, tannins, and body)*

NOTES

Place Label Here.

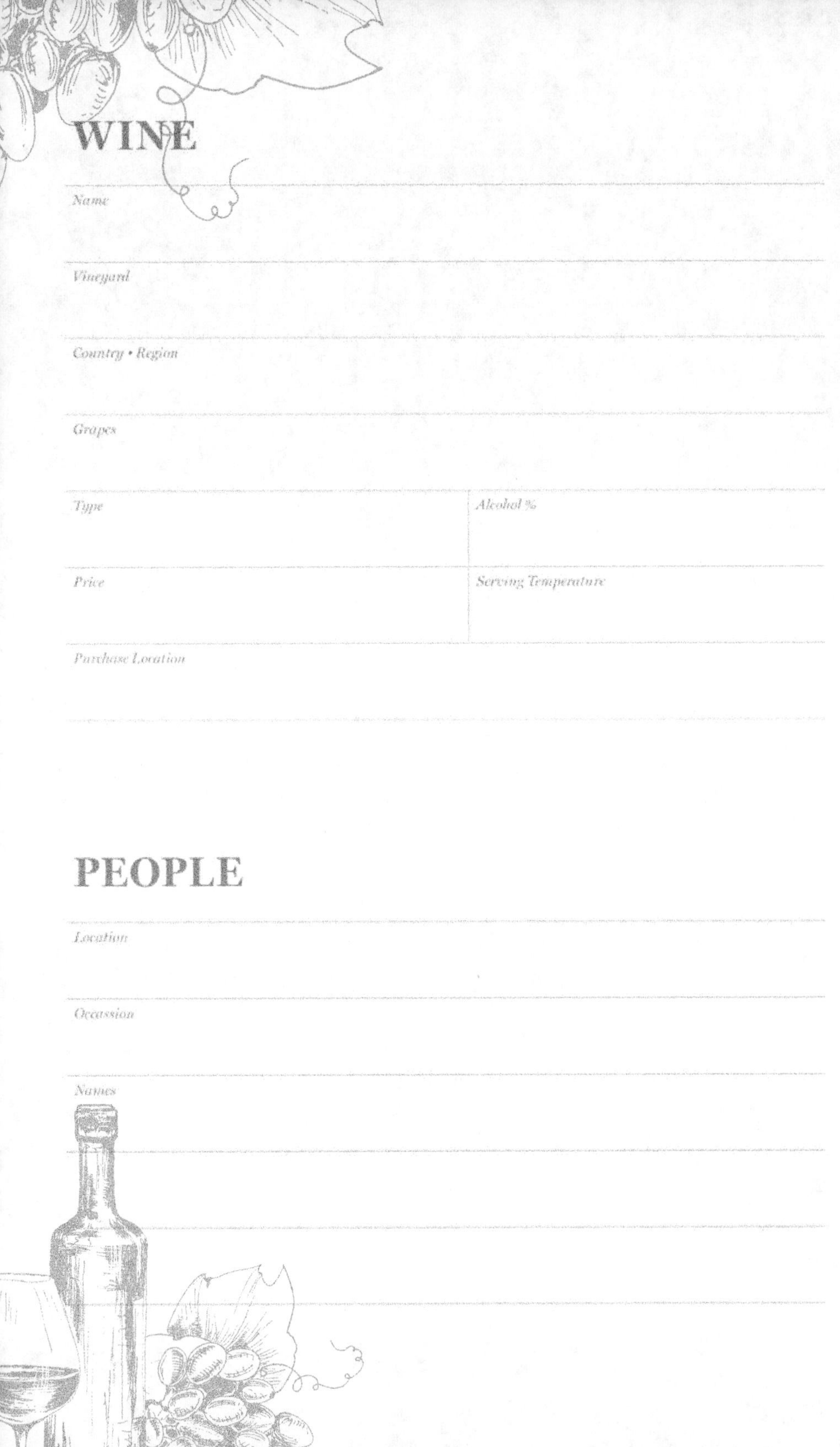

WINE

Name

Vineyard

Country • Region

Grapes

Type	Alcohol %
Price	Serving Temperature

Purchase Location

PEOPLE

Location

Occassion

Names

APPEARANCE *(Circle One)*

RED	Purple	Ruby	Garnet	Tawny	Brick
WHITE	Amber	Pink	Gold	Brown	Yellow
ROSE	Red	Pink	Salmon	Copper	Orange

AROMA *(Describe smell such as fruits, herbs, and spices)*

TASTE *(Describe the sweetness, acidity, tannins, and body)*

NOTES

Place Label Here.

WINE

Name

Vineyard

Country • Region

Grapes

Type

Alcohol %

Price

Serving Temperature

Purchase Location

PEOPLE

Location

Occassion

Names

APPEARANCE *(Circle One)*

RED	Purple	Ruby	Garnet	Tawny	Brick
WHITE	Amber	Pink	Gold	Brown	Yellow
ROSE	Red	Pink	Salmon	Copper	Orange

AROMA *(Describe smell such as fruits, herbs, and spices)*

TASTE *(Describe the sweetness, acidity, tannins, and body)*

NOTES

Place Label Here.

WINE

Name

Vineyard

Country • Region

Grapes

Type	Alcohol %
Price	Serving Temperature

Purchase Location

PEOPLE

Location

Occassion

Names

APPEARANCE *(Circle One)*

RED	Purple	Ruby	Garnet	Tawny	Brick
WHITE	Amber	Pink	Gold	Brown	Yellow
ROSE	Red	Pink	Salmon	Copper	Orange

AROMA *(Describe smell such as fruits, herbs, and spices)*

TASTE *(Describe the sweetness, acidity, tannins, and body)*

NOTES

Place Label Here.

WINE

Name

Vineyard

Country • Region

Grapes

Type	*Alcohol %*
Price	*Serving Temperature*

Purchase Location

PEOPLE

Location

Occassion

Names

APPEARANCE *(Circle One)*

RED	Purple	Ruby	Garnet	Tawny	Brick
WHITE	Amber	Pink	Gold	Brown	Yellow
ROSE	Red	Pink	Salmon	Copper	Orange

AROMA *(Describe smell such as fruits, herbs, and spices)*

TASTE *(Describe the sweetness, acidity, tannins, and body)*

NOTES

Place Label Here.

WINE

Name

Vineyard

Country • Region

Grapes

Type

Alcohol %

Price

Serving Temperature

Purchase Location

PEOPLE

Location

Occassion

Names

APPEARANCE *(Circle One)*

RED	Purple	Ruby	Garnet	Tawny	Brick
WHITE	Amber	Pink	Gold	Brown	Yellow
ROSE	Red	Pink	Salmon	Copper	Orange

AROMA *(Describe smell such as fruits, herbs, and spices)*

TASTE *(Describe the sweetness, acidity, tannins, and body)*

NOTES

Place Label Here.

WINE

Name

Vineyard

Country • Region

Grapes

Type	Alcohol %
Price	Serving Temperature

Purchase Location

PEOPLE

Location

Occasion

Names

APPEARANCE *(Circle One)*

RED	Purple	Ruby	Garnet	Tawny	Brick
WHITE	Amber	Pink	Gold	Brown	Yellow
ROSE	Red	Pink	Salmon	Copper	Orange

AROMA *(Describe smell such as fruits, herbs, and spices)*

TASTE *(Describe the sweetness, acidity, tannins, and body)*

NOTES

Place Label Here.

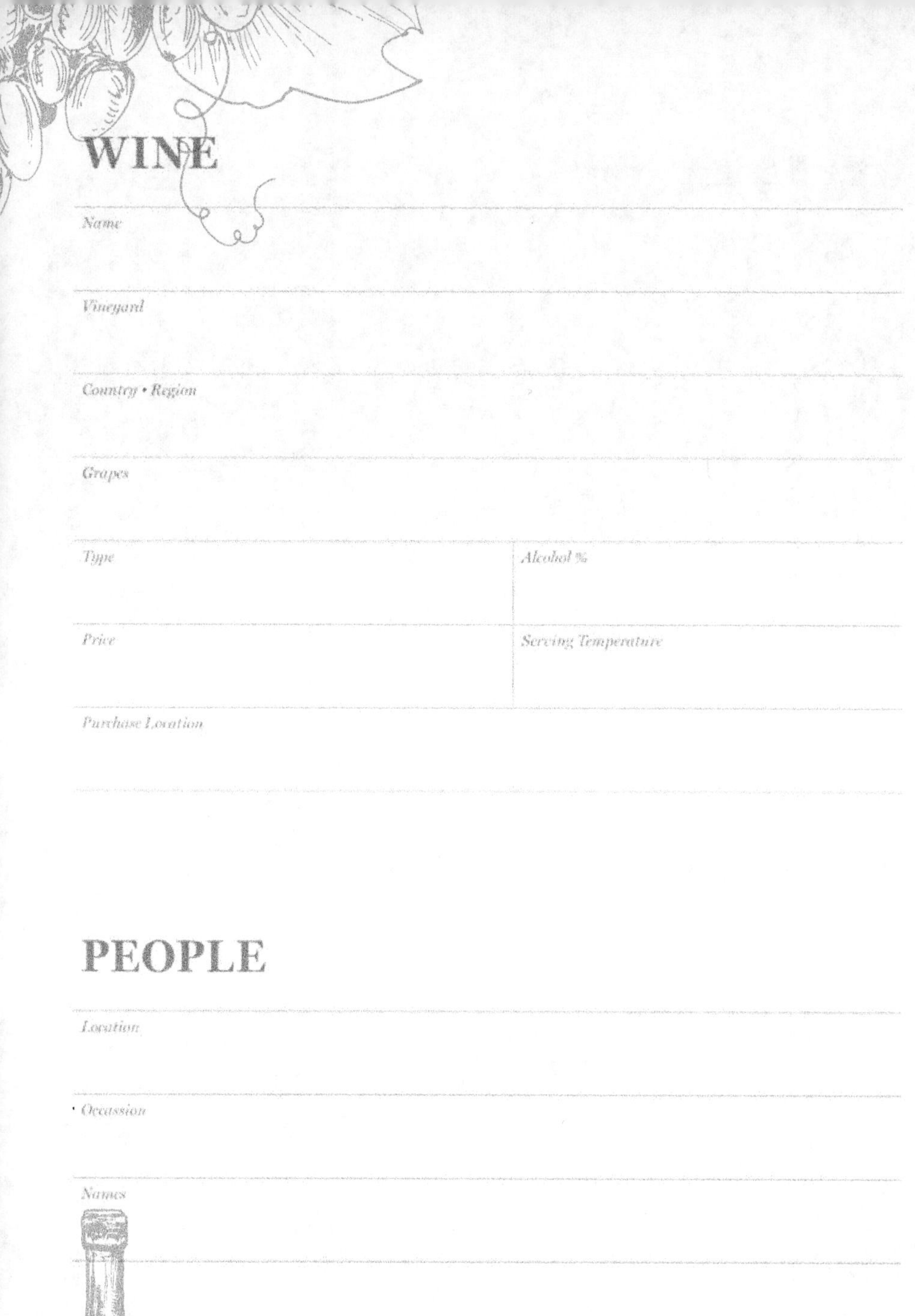

WINE

Name

Vineyard

Country • Region

Grapes

Type	*Alcohol %*
Price	*Serving Temperature*

Purchase Location

PEOPLE

Location

• *Occassion*

Names

APPEARANCE *(Circle One)*

RED	Purple	Ruby	Garnet	Tawny	Brick
WHITE	Amber	Pink	Gold	Brown	Yellow
ROSE	Red	Pink	Salmon	Copper	Orange

____

____

____

AROMA *(Describe smell such as fruits, herbs, and spices)*

____

____

____

____

TASTE *(Describe the sweetness, acidity, tannins, and body)*

NOTES

Place Label Here.

WINE

Name

Vineyard

Country • Region

Grapes

Type	Alcohol %
Price	Serving Temperature

Purchase Location

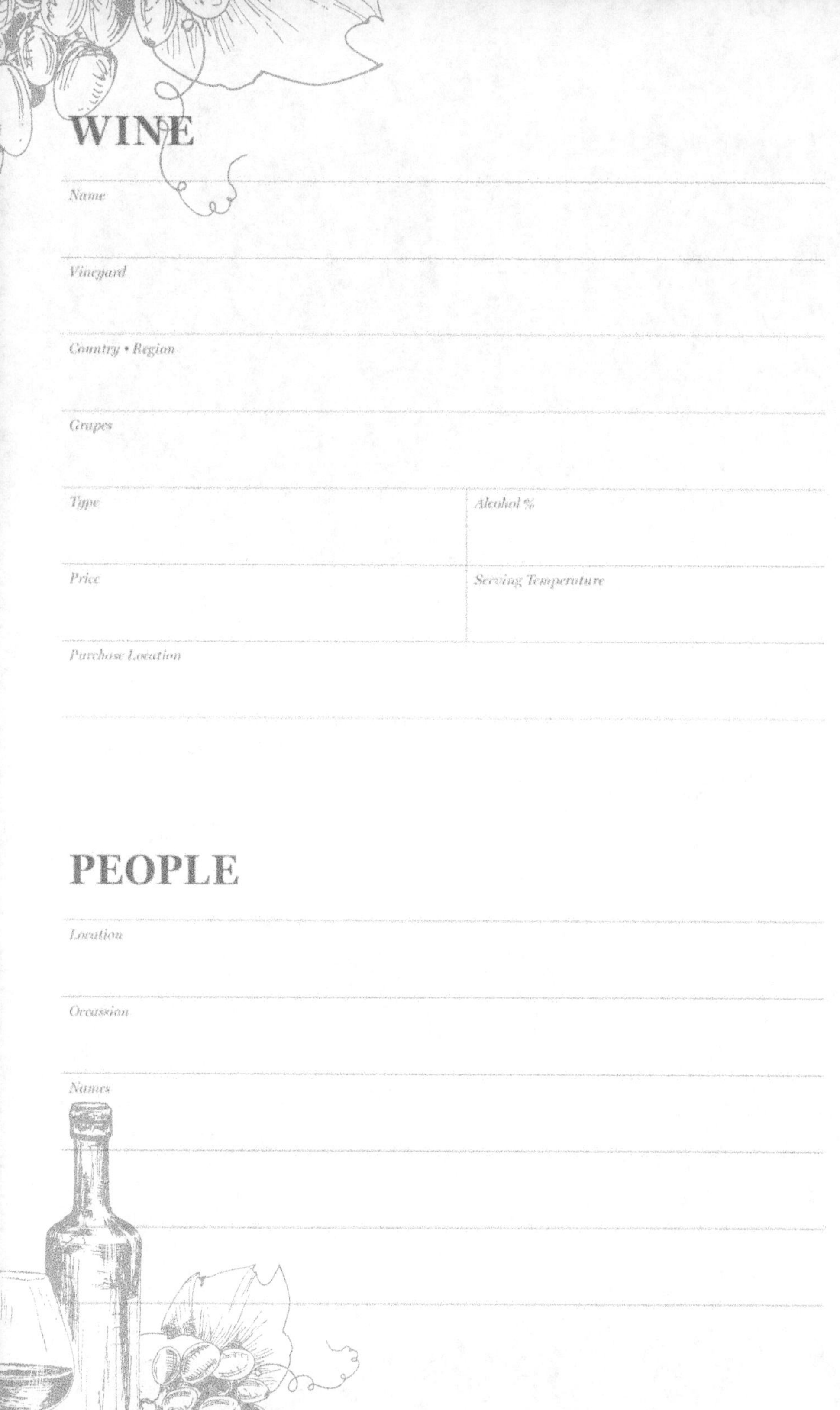

PEOPLE

Location

Occassion

Names

APPEARANCE *(Circle One)*

RED	Purple	Ruby	Garnet	Tawny	Brick
WHITE	Amber	Pink	Gold	Brown	Yellow
ROSE	Red	Pink	Salmon	Copper	Orange

AROMA *(Describe smell such as fruits, herbs, and spices)*

TASTE *(Describe the sweetness, acidity, tannins, and body)*

NOTES

Place Label Here.

WINE

Name

Vineyard

Country • Region

Grapes

Type

Alcohol %

Price

Serving Temperature

Purchase Location

PEOPLE

Location

Occasion

Names

APPEARANCE *(Circle One)*

RED	Purple	Ruby	Garnet	Tawny	Brick
WHITE	Amber	Pink	Gold	Brown	Yellow
ROSE	Red	Pink	Salmon	Copper	Orange

AROMA *(Describe smell such as fruits, herbs, and spices)*

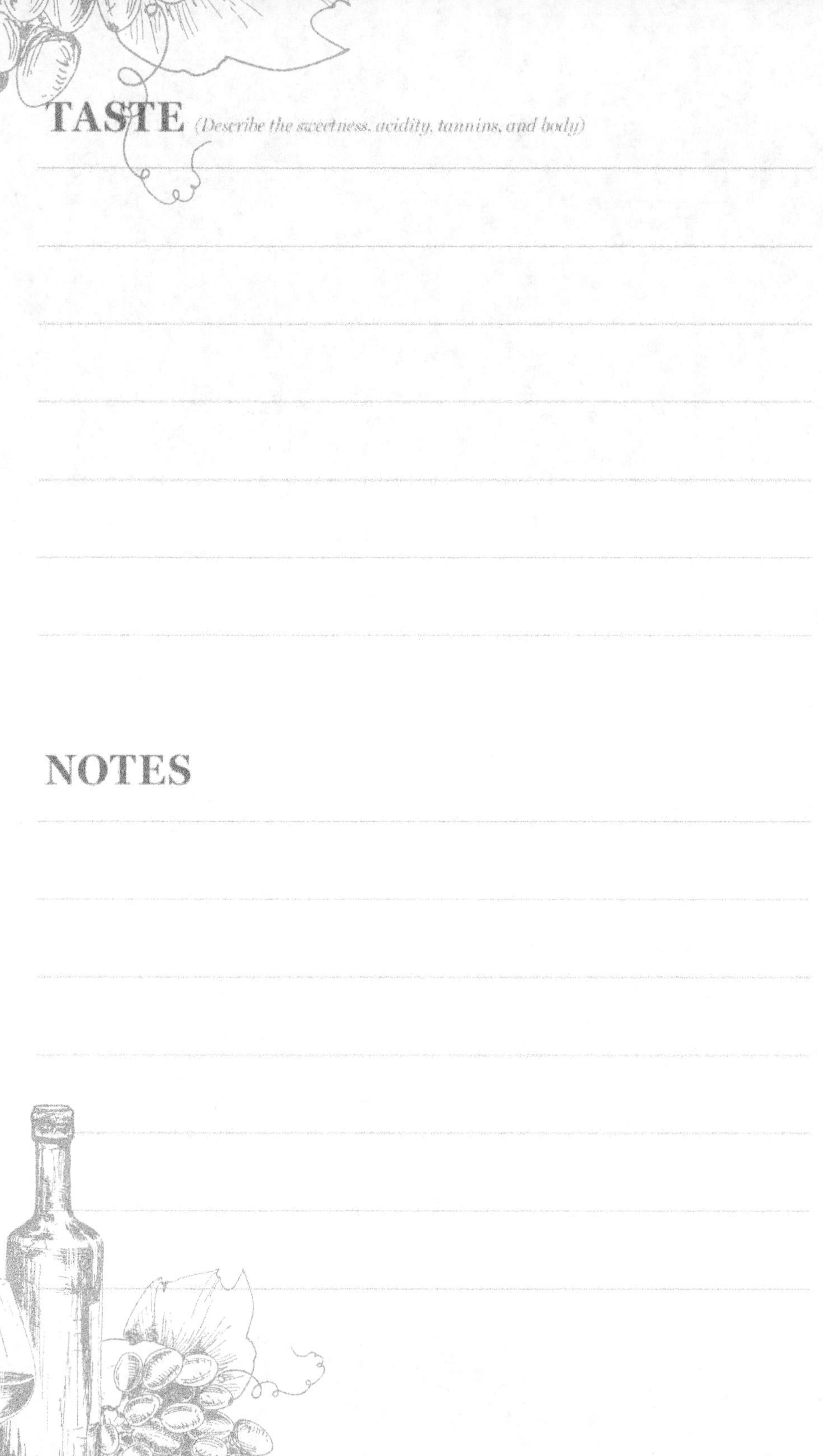

TASTE *(Describe the sweetness, acidity, tannins, and body)*

NOTES

Place Label Here.

WINE

Name

Vineyard

Country • Region

Grapes

Type	Alcohol %
Price	Serving Temperature

Purchase Location

PEOPLE

Location

Occassion

Names

APPEARANCE *(Circle One)*

RED	Purple	Ruby	Garnet	Tawny	Brick
WHITE	Amber	Pink	Gold	Brown	Yellow
ROSE	Red	Pink	Salmon	Copper	Orange

AROMA *(Describe smell such as fruits, herbs, and spices)*

NOTES

Place Label Here.

WINE

Name

Vineyard

Country • Region

Grapes

Type

Alcohol %

Price

Serving Temperature

Purchase Location

PEOPLE

Location

Occassion

Names

APPEARANCE *(Circle One)*

RED	Purple	Ruby	Garnet	Tawny	Brick
WHITE	Amber	Pink	Gold	Brown	Yellow
ROSE	Red	Pink	Salmon	Copper	Orange

AROMA *(Describe smell such as fruits, herbs, and spices)*

TASTE *(Describe the sweetness, acidity, tannins, and body)*

NOTES

Place Label Here.

WINE

Name

Vineyard

Country • Region

Grapes

Type

Alcohol %

Price

Serving Temperature

Purchase Location

PEOPLE

Location

Occasion

Names

APPEARANCE *(Circle One)*

RED	Purple	Ruby	Garnet	Tawny	Brick
WHITE	Amber	Pink	Gold	Brown	Yellow
ROSE	Red	Pink	Salmon	Copper	Orange

AROMA *(Describe smell such as fruits, herbs, and spices)*

TASTE *(Describe the sweetness, acidity, tannins, and body)*

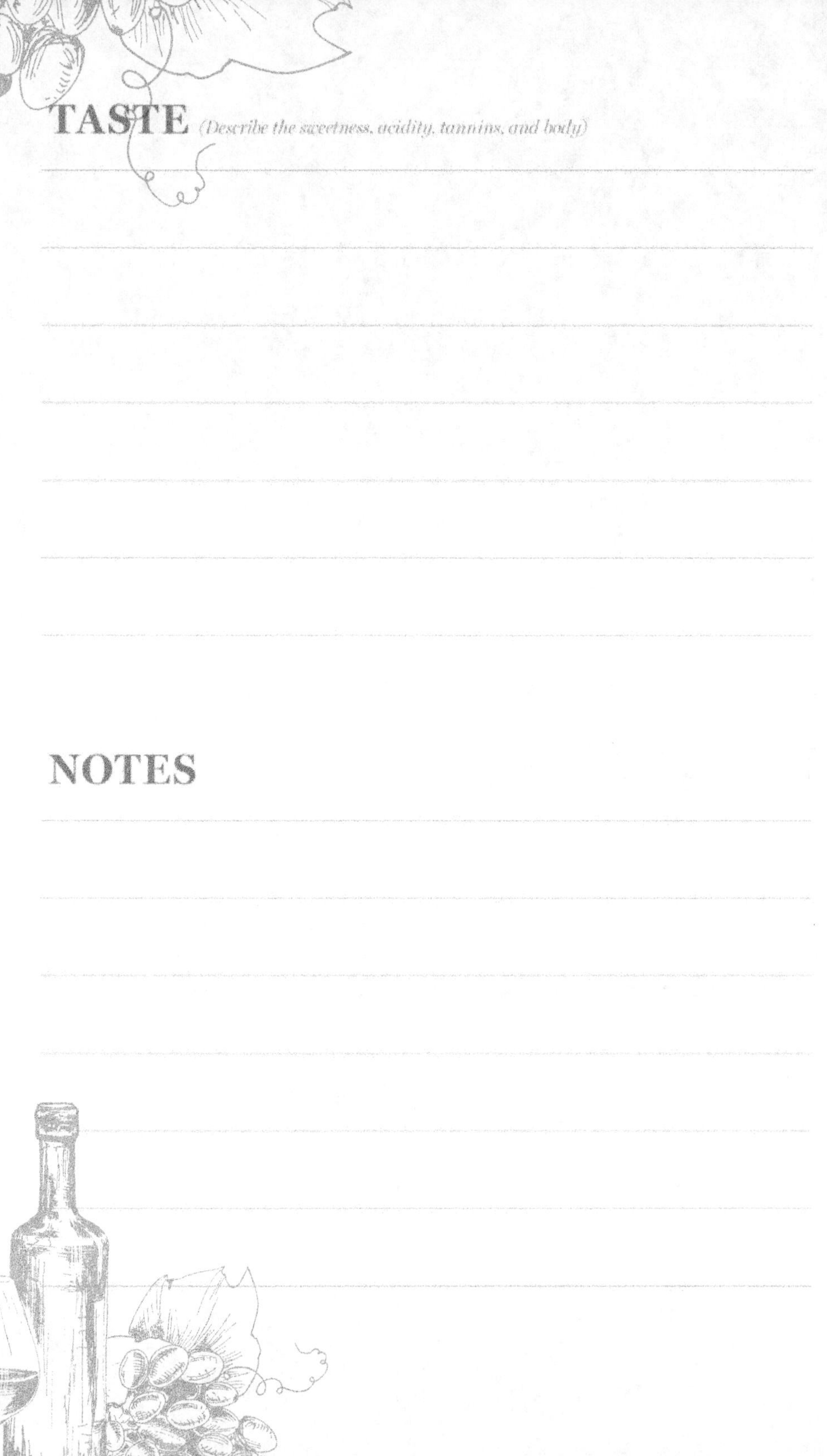

NOTES

Place Label Here.

WINE

Name

Vineyard

Country • Region

Grapes

Type	*Alcohol %*
Price	*Serving Temperature*

Purchase Location

PEOPLE

Location

Occasion

Names

APPEARANCE *(Circle One)*

RED	Purple	Ruby	Garnet	Tawny	Brick
WHITE	Amber	Pink	Gold	Brown	Yellow
ROSE	Red	Pink	Salmon	Copper	Orange

AROMA *(Describe smell such as fruits, herbs, and spices)*

TASTE *(Describe the sweetness, acidity, tannins, and body)*

NOTES

Place Label Here.

WINE

Name

Vineyard

Country • Region

Grapes

Type	Alcohol %
Price	Serving Temperature

Purchase Location

PEOPLE

Location

Occassion

Names

APPEARANCE *(Circle One)*

RED	Purple	Ruby	Garnet	Tawny	Brick
WHITE	Amber	Pink	Gold	Brown	Yellow
ROSE	Red	Pink	Salmon	Copper	Orange

AROMA *(Describe smell such as fruits, herbs, and spices)*

TASTE *(Describe the sweetness, acidity, tannins, and body)*

NOTES

Place Label Here.

WINE

Name

Vineyard

Country • Region

Grapes

Type	Alcohol %
Price	Serving Temperature

Purchase Location

PEOPLE

Location

Occasion

Names

APPEARANCE *(Circle One)*

RED	Purple	Ruby	Garnet	Tawny	Brick
WHITE	Amber	Pink	Gold	Brown	Yellow
ROSE	Red	Pink	Salmon	Copper	Orange

AROMA *(Describe smell such as fruits, herbs, and spices)*

TASTE *(Describe the sweetness, acidity, tannins, and body)*

NOTES

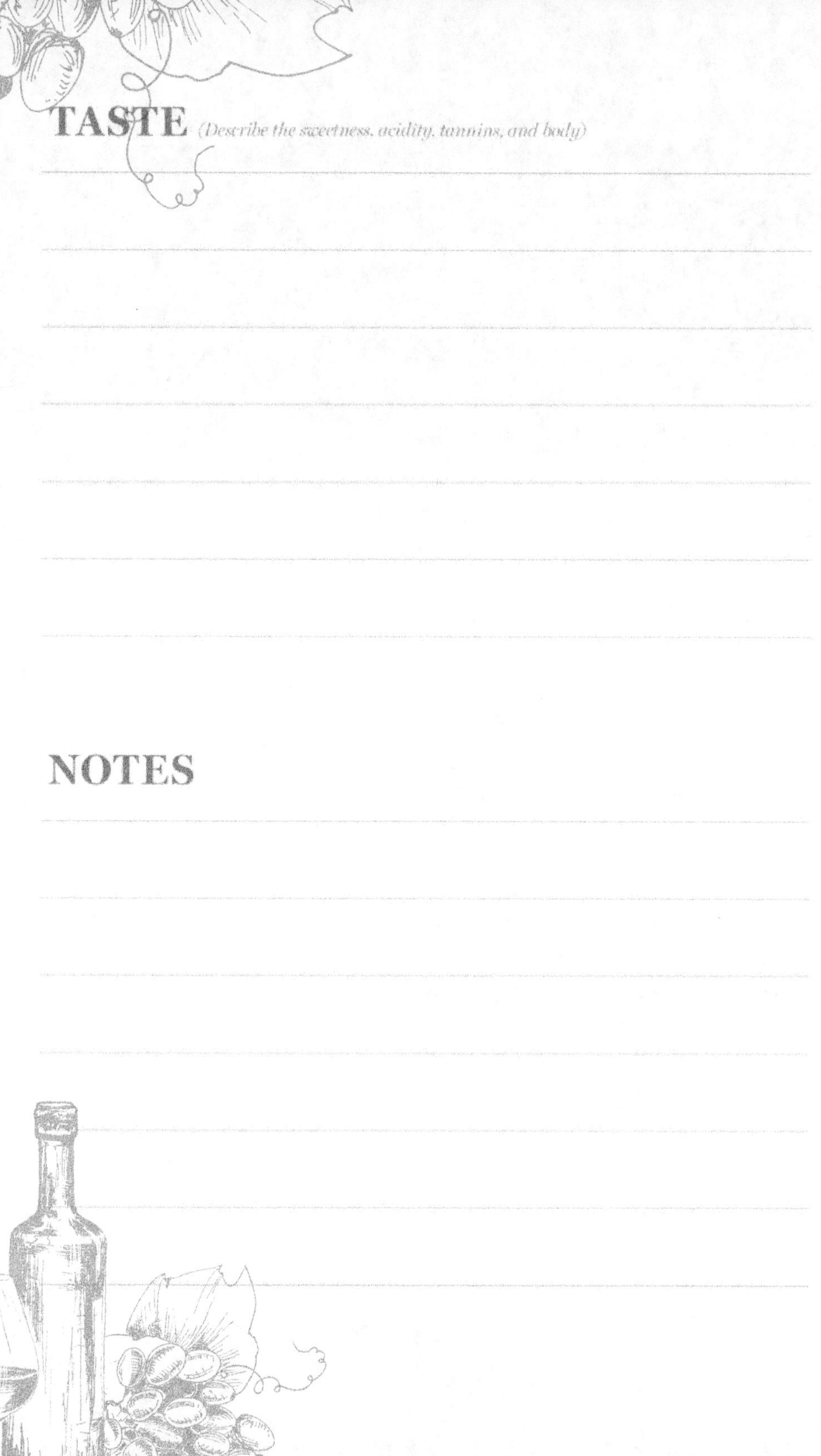

Place Label Here.

WINE

Name

Vineyard

Country • Region

Grapes

Type	Alcohol %
Price	Serving Temperature

Purchase Location

PEOPLE

Location

Occassion

Names

APPEARANCE *(Circle One)*

RED	Purple	Ruby	Garnet	Tawny	Brick
WHITE	Amber	Pink	Gold	Brown	Yellow
ROSE	Red	Pink	Salmon	Copper	Orange

AROMA *(Describe smell such as fruits, herbs, and spices)*

TASTE *(Describe the sweetness, acidity, tannins, and body)*

NOTES

Place Label Here.

WINE

Name

Vineyard

Country • Region

Grapes

Type	*Alcohol %*
Price	*Serving Temperature*

Purchase Location

PEOPLE

Location

Occassion

Names

APPEARANCE *(Circle One)*

RED	Purple	Ruby	Garnet	Tawny	Brick
WHITE	Amber	Pink	Gold	Brown	Yellow
ROSE	Red	Pink	Salmon	Copper	Orange

AROMA *(Describe smell such as fruits, herbs, and spices)*

TASTE *(Describe the sweetness, acidity, tannins, and body)*

NOTES

Place Label Here.

WINE

Name

Vineyard

Country • Region

Grapes

Type

Alcohol %

Price

Serving Temperature

Purchase Location

PEOPLE

Location

Occassion

Names

APPEARANCE *(Circle One)*

RED	Purple	Ruby	Garnet	Tawny	Brick
WHITE	Amber	Pink	Gold	Brown	Yellow
ROSE	Red	Pink	Salmon	Copper	Orange

AROMA *(Describe smell such as fruits, herbs, and spices)*

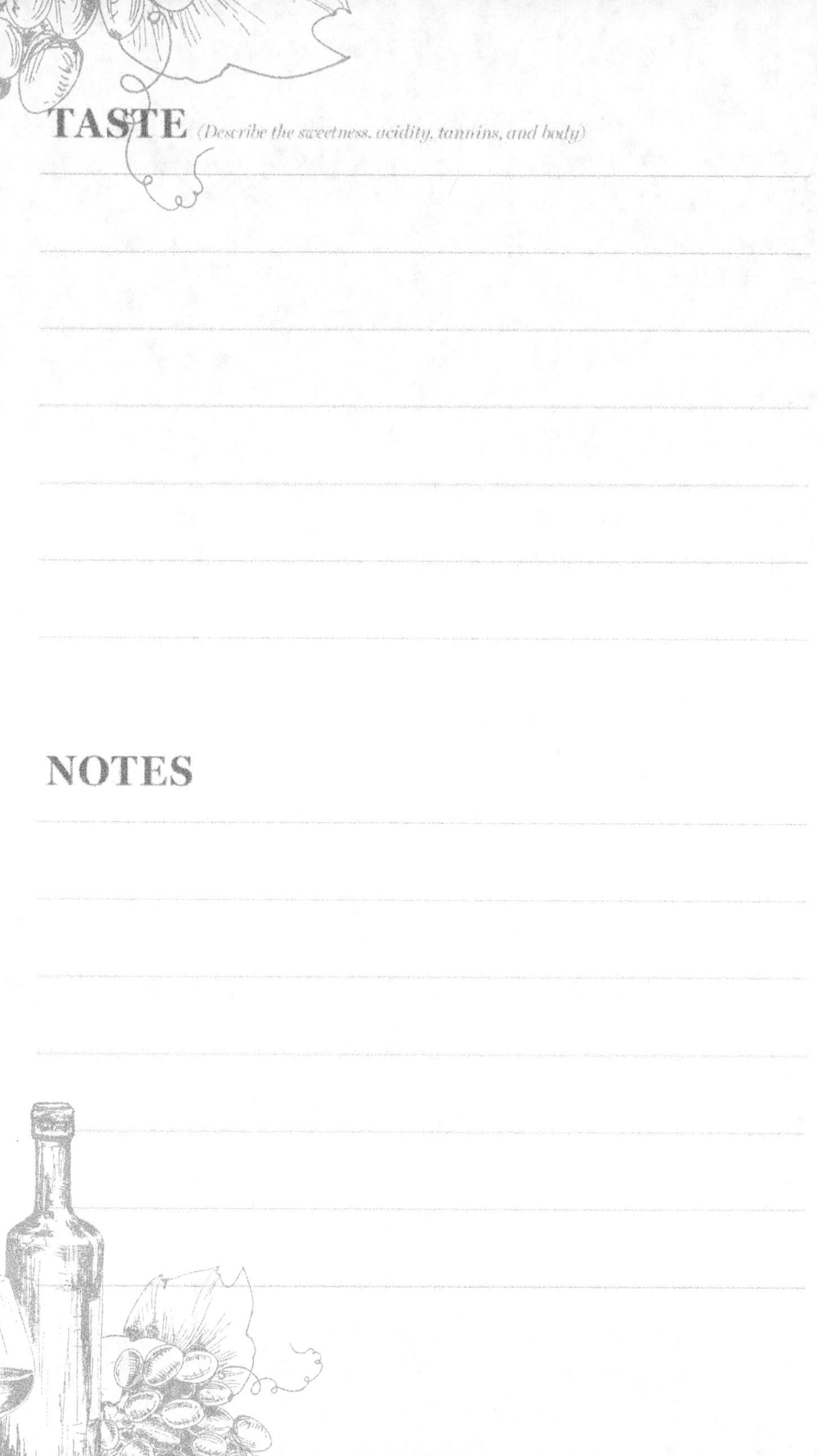

TASTE *(Describe the sweetness, acidity, tannins, and body)*

NOTES

Place Label Here.

WINE

Name

Vineyard

Country • Region

Grapes

Type	*Alcohol ‰*
Price	*Serving Temperature*

Purchase Location

PEOPLE

Location

Occassion

Names

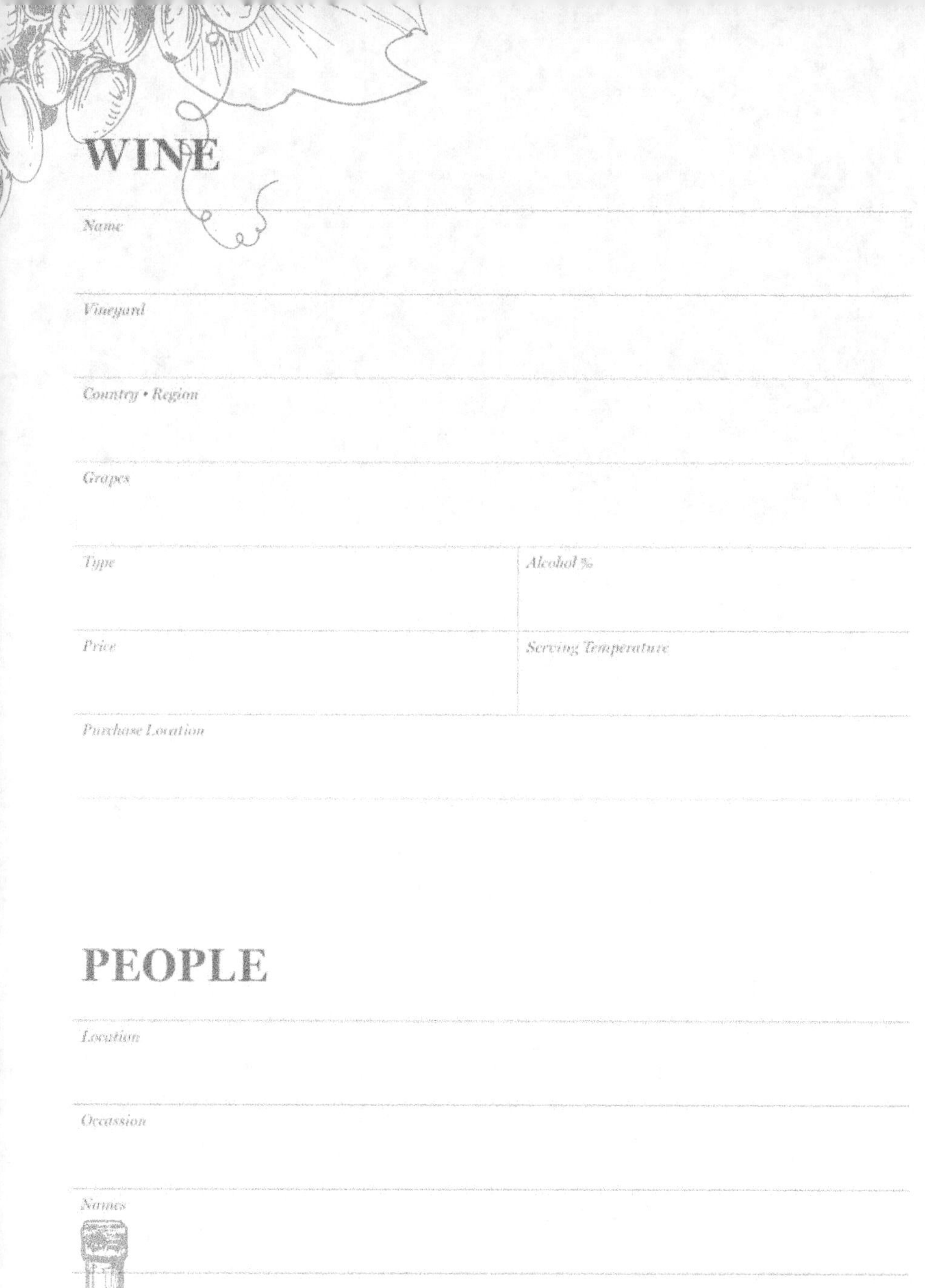

APPEARANCE *(Circle One)*

RED	Purple	Ruby	Garnet	Tawny	Brick
WHITE	Amber	Pink	Gold	Brown	Yellow
ROSE	Red	Pink	Salmon	Copper	Orange

AROMA *(Describe smell such as fruits, herbs, and spices)*

TASTE *(Describe the sweetness, acidity, tannins, and body)*

NOTES

Place Label Here.

WINE

Name

Vineyard

Country • Region

Grapes

Type

Alcohol %

Price

Serving Temperature

Purchase Location

PEOPLE

Location

Occassion

Names

APPEARANCE *(Circle One)*

RED	Purple	Ruby	Garnet	Tawny	Brick
WHITE	Amber	Pink	Gold	Brown	Yellow
ROSE	Red	Pink	Salmon	Copper	Orange

AROMA *(Describe smell such as fruits, herbs, and spices)*

TASTE *(Describe the sweetness, acidity, tannins, and body)*

NOTES

Place Label Here.

WINE

Name

Vineyard

Country • Region

Grapes

Type	Alcohol %
Price	Serving Temperature

Purchase Location

PEOPLE

Location

Occasion

Names

APPEARANCE *(Circle One)*

RED	Purple	Ruby	Garnet	Tawny	Brick
WHITE	Amber	Pink	Gold	Brown	Yellow
ROSE	Red	Pink	Salmon	Copper	Orange

AROMA *(Describe smell such as fruits, herbs, and spices)*

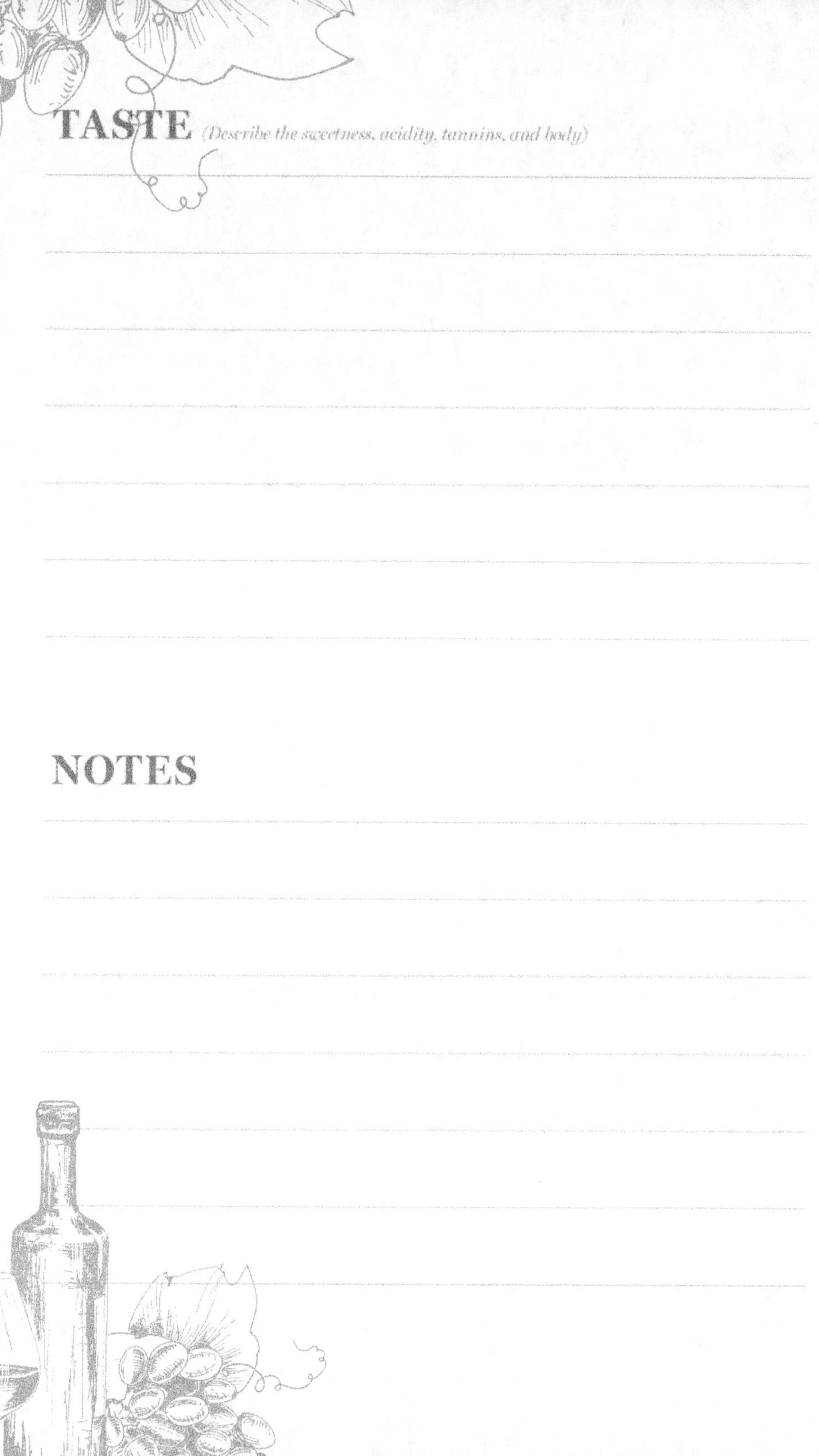

TASTE *(Describe the sweetness, acidity, tannins, and body)*

NOTES

Place Label Here.

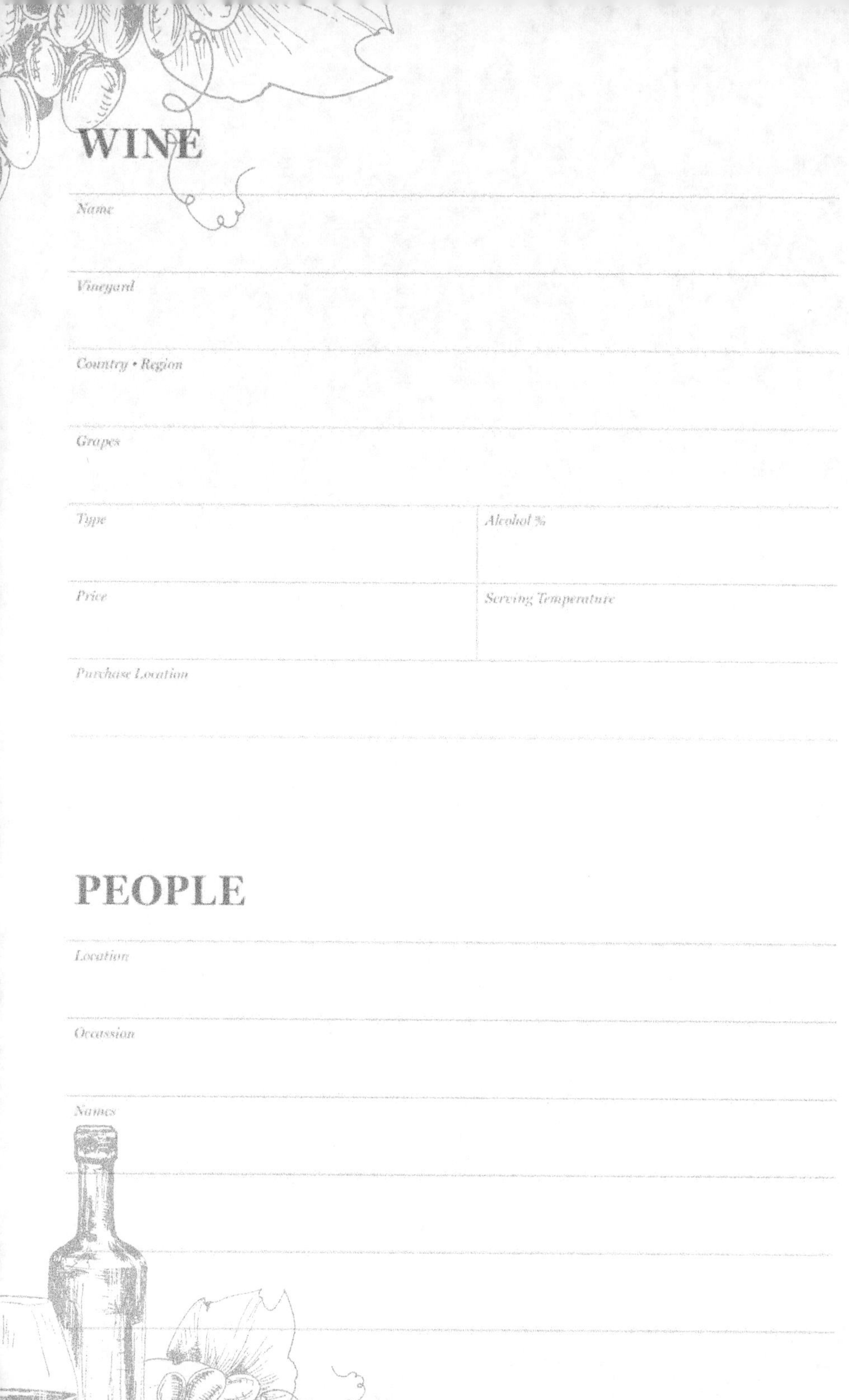

WINE

Name

Vineyard

Country • Region

Grapes

Type

Alcohol %

Price

Serving Temperature

Purchase Location

PEOPLE

Location

Occassion

Names

APPEARANCE *(Circle One)*

RED	Purple	Ruby	Garnet	Tawny	Brick
WHITE	Amber	Pink	Gold	Brown	Yellow
ROSE	Red	Pink	Salmon	Copper	Orange

AROMA *(Describe smell such as fruits, herbs, and spices)*

TASTE *(Describe the sweetness, acidity, tannins, and body)*

NOTES

Place Label Here.

WINE

Name

Vineyard

Country • Region

Grapes

Type	*Alcohol %*
Price	*Serving Temperature*

Purchase Location

PEOPLE

Location

Occassion

Names

APPEARANCE *(Circle One)*

RED	Purple	Ruby	Garnet	Tawny	Brick
WHITE	Amber	Pink	Gold	Brown	Yellow
ROSE	Red	Pink	Salmon	Copper	Orange

AROMA *(Describe smell such as fruits, herbs, and spices)*

TASTE *(Describe the sweetness, acidity, tannins, and body)*

NOTES

Place Label Here.

WINE

Name

Vineyard

Country • Region

Grapes

Type	Alcohol %
Price	Serving Temperature

Purchase Location

PEOPLE

Location

Occassion

Names

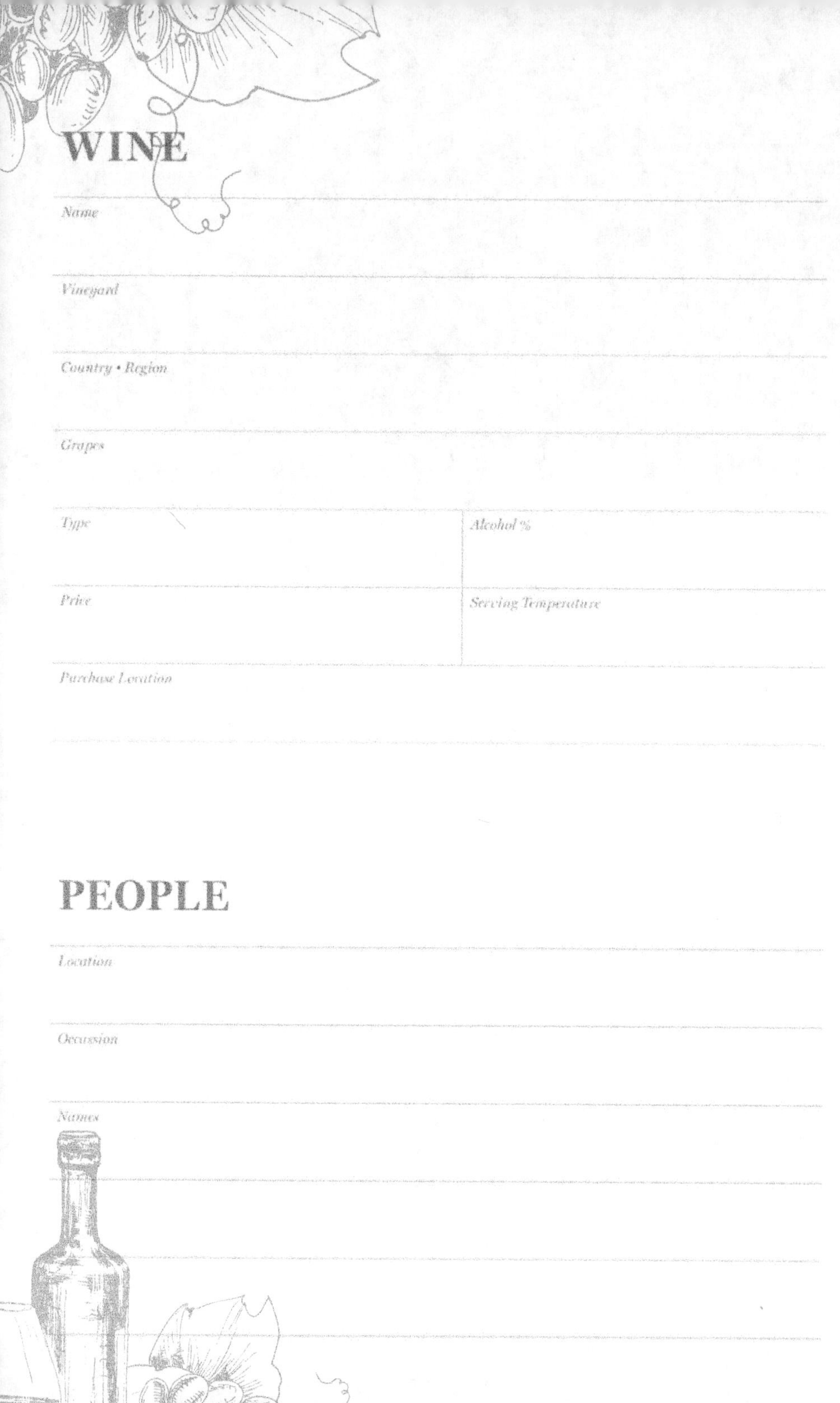

APPEARANCE *(Circle One)*

RED	Purple	Ruby	Garnet	Tawny	Brick
WHITE	Amber	Pink	Gold	Brown	Yellow
ROSE	Red	Pink	Salmon	Copper	Orange

AROMA *(Describe smell such as fruits, herbs, and spices)*

TASTE *(Describe the sweetness, acidity, tannins, and body)*

NOTES

Place Label Here.

WINE

Name

Vineyard

Country • Region

Grapes

Type	Alcohol %
Price	Serving Temperature

Purchase Location

PEOPLE

Location

Occassion

Names

APPEARANCE *(Circle One)*

RED	Purple	Ruby	Garnet	Tawny	Brick
WHITE	Amber	Pink	Gold	Brown	Yellow
ROSE	Red	Pink	Salmon	Copper	Orange

AROMA *(Describe smell such as fruits, herbs, and spices)*

TASTE *(Describe the sweetness, acidity, tannins, and body)*

NOTES

Place Label Here.

WINE

Name

Vineyard

Country • Region

Grapes

Type	Alcohol %
Price	Serving Temperature

Purchase Location

PEOPLE

Location

Occassion

Names

APPEARANCE *(Circle One)*

RED	Purple	Ruby	Garnet	Tawny	Brick
WHITE	Amber	Pink	Gold	Brown	Yellow
ROSE	Red	Pink	Salmon	Copper	Orange

AROMA *(Describe smell such as fruits, herbs, and spices)*

TASTE *(Describe the sweetness, acidity, tannins, and body)*

NOTES

Place Label Here.

WINE

Name

Vineyard

Country • Region

Grapes

Type	Alcohol %
Price	Serving Temperature

Purchase Location

PEOPLE

Location

Occassion

Names

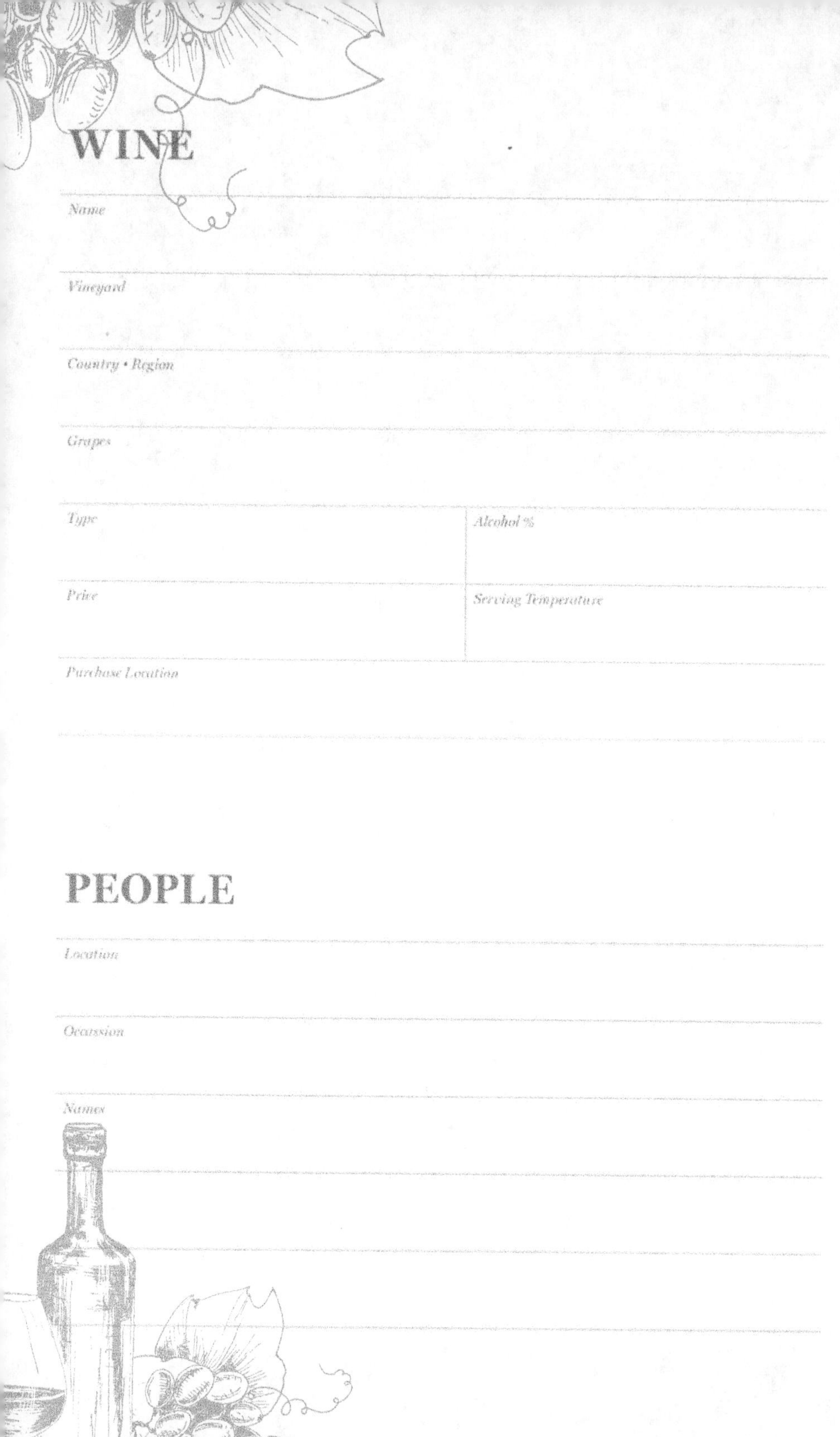

APPEARANCE (Circle One)

RED	Purple	Ruby	Garnet	Tawny	Brick
WHITE	Amber	Pink	Gold	Brown	Yellow
ROSE	Red	Pink	Salmon	Copper	Orange

AROMA (Describe smell such as fruits, herbs, and spices)

TASTE *(Describe the sweetness, acidity, tannins, and body)*

NOTES

Place Label Here.

WINE

Name

Vineyard

Country • Region

Grapes

Type	*Alcohol %*
Price	*Serving Temperature*

Purchase Location

PEOPLE

Location

Occassion

Names

APPEARANCE *(Circle One)*

RED	Purple	Ruby	Garnet	Tawny	Brick
WHITE	Amber	Pink	Gold	Brown	Yellow
ROSE	Red	Pink	Salmon	Copper	Orange

AROMA *(Describe smell such as fruits, herbs, and spices)*

TASTE *(Describe the sweetness, acidity, tannins, and body)*

NOTES

Place Label Here.

WINE

Name

Vineyard

Country • Region

Grapes

Type	*Alcohol %*
Price	*Serving Temperature*

Purchase Location

PEOPLE

Location

Occassion

Names

APPEARANCE *(Circle One)*

RED	Purple	Ruby	Garnet	Tawny	Brick
WHITE	Amber	Pink	Gold	Brown	Yellow
ROSE	Red	Pink	Salmon	Copper	Orange

AROMA *(Describe smell such as fruits, herbs, and spices)*

TASTE *(Describe the sweetness, acidity, tannins, and body)*

NOTES

Place Label Here.

WINE

Name

Vineyard

Country • Region

Grapes

Type	*Alcohol %*
Price	*Serving Temperature*

Purchase Location

PEOPLE

Location

Occasion

Names

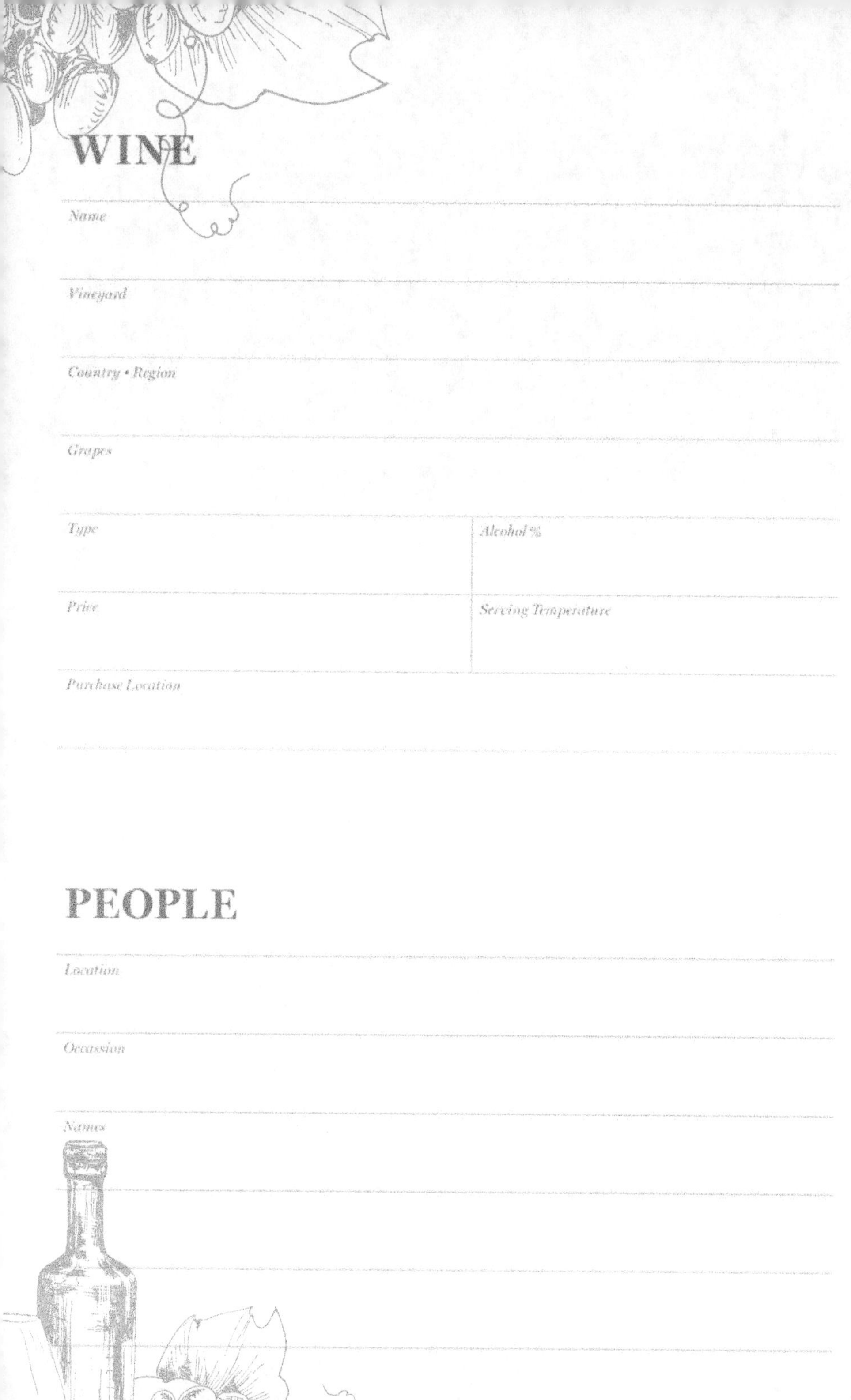

APPEARANCE *(Circle One)*

RED	Purple	Ruby	Garnet	Tawny	Brick
WHITE	Amber	Pink	Gold	Brown	Yellow
ROSE	Red	Pink	Salmon	Copper	Orange

AROMA *(Describe smell such as fruits, herbs, and spices)*

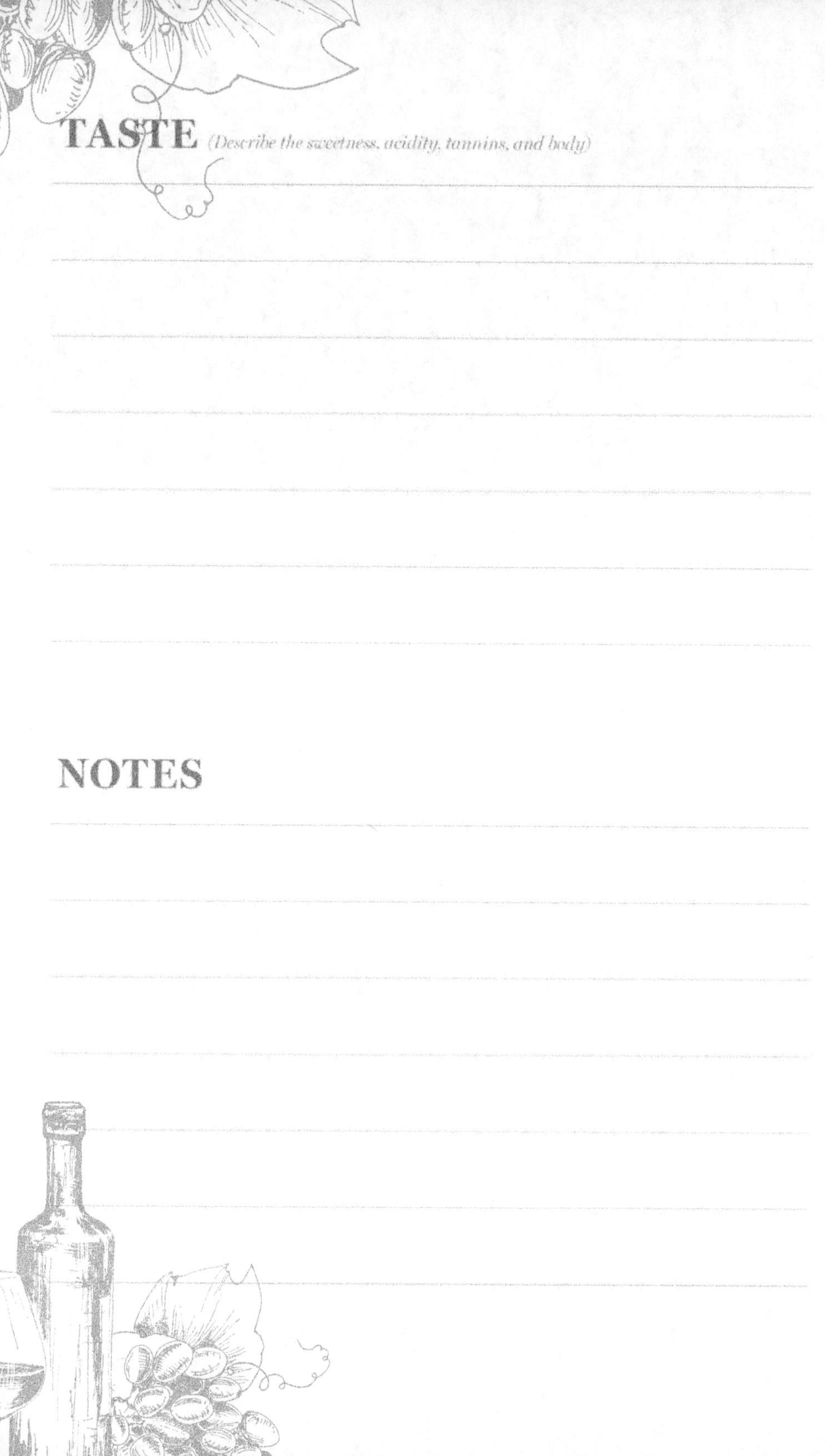

TASTE *(Describe the sweetness, acidity, tannins, and body)*

NOTES

Place Label Here.

WINE

Name

Vineyard

Country • Region

Grapes

Type

Alcohol %

Price

Serving Temperature

Purchase Location

PEOPLE

Location

Occassion

Names

APPEARANCE *(Circle One)*

RED	Purple	Ruby	Garnet	Tawny	Brick
WHITE	Amber	Pink	Gold	Brown	Yellow
ROSE	Red	Pink	Salmon	Copper	Orange

AROMA *(Describe smell such as fruits, herbs, and spices)*

TASTE *(Describe the sweetness, acidity, tannins, and body)*

NOTES

Place Label Here.

WINE

Name

Vineyard

Country • Region

Grapes

Type

Alcohol %

Price

Serving Temperature

Purchase Location

PEOPLE

Location

Occassion

Names

APPEARANCE *(Circle One)*

RED	Purple	Ruby	Garnet	Tawny	Brick
WHITE	Amber	Pink	Gold	Brown	Yellow
ROSE	Red	Pink	Salmon	Copper	Orange

AROMA *(Describe smell such as fruits, herbs, and spices)*

TASTE *(Describe the sweetness, acidity, tannins, and body)*

NOTES

Place Label Here.

WINE

Name

Vineyard

Country • Region

Grapes

Type	Alcohol %
Price	Serving Temperature

Purchase Location

PEOPLE

Location

Occassion

Names

APPEARANCE *(Circle One)*

RED	Purple	Ruby	Garnet	Tawny	Brick
WHITE	Amber	Pink	Gold	Brown	Yellow
ROSE	Red	Pink	Salmon	Copper	Orange

AROMA *(Describe smell such as fruits, herbs, and spices)*

TASTE *(Describe the sweetness, acidity, tannins, and body)*

NOTES

Place Label Here.

WINE

Name

Vineyard

Country • Region

Grapes

Type	Alcohol %
Price	Serving Temperature

Purchase Location

PEOPLE

Location

Occassion

Names

APPEARANCE *(Circle One)*

RED	Purple	Ruby	Garnet	Tawny	Brick
WHITE	Amber	Pink	Gold	Brown	Yellow
ROSE	Red	Pink	Salmon	Copper	Orange

AROMA *(Describe smell such as fruits, herbs, and spices)*

TASTE *(Describe the sweetness, acidity, tannins, and body)*

NOTES

Place Label Here.

WINE

Name

Vineyard

Country • Region

Grapes

Type

Alcohol %

Price

Serving Temperature

Purchase Location

PEOPLE

Location

Occassion

Names

APPEARANCE *(Circle One)*

RED	Purple	Ruby	Garnet	Tawny	Brick
WHITE	Amber	Pink	Gold	Brown	Yellow
ROSE	Red	Pink	Salmon	Copper	Orange

AROMA *(Describe smell such as fruits, herbs, and spices)*

TASTE *(Describe the sweetness, acidity, tannins, and body)*

NOTES

CREATEPUBLICATION

Thank you!

As a small family company, your feedback is very
important to us.
Please let us know how you like our book at:

/createpublication
/createpublication
createpublication@gmail.com

www.ingramcontent.com/pod-product-compliance
Lightning Source LLC
Chambersburg PA
CBHW060934050726
47592CB00003B/951